I0867349

KNIT CAKERY

10 FUN PROJECTS
USING YARN CAKES

LEISURE ARTS, INC. • Maumelle, Arkansas

Contents

LION BRAND® AMAZING LACE

Easy Eyelet Shawl

●●○○ **EASY**

SIZE

About 30 x 84 in. (76 x 213.5 cm), at longest and widest

GAUGE

22 sts = about 4 in. (10 cm) in Garter st (knit every st on every row).

BE SURE TO CHECK YOUR GAUGE.

MATERIALS

Yarn (Super Fine) SUPER FINE 1

Lion Brand® AMAZING LACE (Art. #213)

☐ #110 Cobalt Butterfly 1 cake

☐ Lion Brand® large-eyed blunt needle

Additional Materials

Circular knitting needle size 5 (3.75 mm), 36 in. (91.5 cm) long

NOTES

1. Shawl is worked in one piece in Garter st (knit every st on every row) and shaped to make an asymmetric triangle.
2. The first st of every row is slipped for a neat edge. Slip the st as if to knit or as if to purl, whichever you prefer.
3. Increases are worked at the beginning of RS rows and end of WS rows and decreases are worked at the end of RS rows to shape the Shawl.
4. A circular needle is used to accommodate the large number of sts. Work back and forth on the circular needle as if you were working on straight needles.
5. For those who find a visual helpful, we have included a chart.

STITCH EXPLANATIONS

kfb (knit in front and back)

Knit next st without removing it from left hand needle, then k through back of same st – 1 st increased.

yo (yarn over)

An increase that also creates a small decorative hole (eyelet) in the fabric, worked as follows:

1. Bring yarn to front, between the needles.

2. Take yarn to back, over the right hand needle. This creates the new st. You are now ready to proceed with the next st as instructed.

SHAWL

Cast on 4 sts.

Row 1 (RS): Sl 1, kfb, k1, p1 – you will have 5 sts in this row.

Row 2: Sl 1, k2tog, kfb, p1 – 5 sts.

Row 3: Sl 1, kfb, k2tog, p1.

Row 4: Sl 1, k to last 2 sts, kfb, p1 – 6 sts.

Row 5: Sl 1, kfb, k to last 3 sts, k2tog, p1.

Row 6: Sl 1, k to last 2 sts, kfb, p1 – 7 sts.

Rows 7-132: Rep Rows 5 and 6 until you have a total of 70 sts.

Begin Lace Section

Row 1 (RS): Sl 1, kfb, k to last 3 sts, k2tog, p1.

Row 2: Sl 1, *yo, k2tog; rep from * to last 3 sts, k1, kfb, p1 – 71 sts.

Row 3: Sl 1, kfb, k to last 3 sts, k2tog, p1.

Row 4: Sl 1, *yo, k2tog; rep from * to last 2 sts, kfb, p1 – 72 sts.

Rows 5-20: Rep Rows 1-4 for 4 more times – 80 sts at the end of Row 20.

Row 21: Sl 1, kfb, k to last 3 sts, k2tog, p1.

Row 22: Sl 1, k to last 2 sts, kfb, p1 – 81 sts.

Rows 23-40: Rep Rows 21 and 22 for 9 times – 90 sts at the end of Row 40.

Rows 41-280: Rep Rows 1-40 for 6 times more – 210 sts.

Bind off.

FINISHING

Weave in ends.

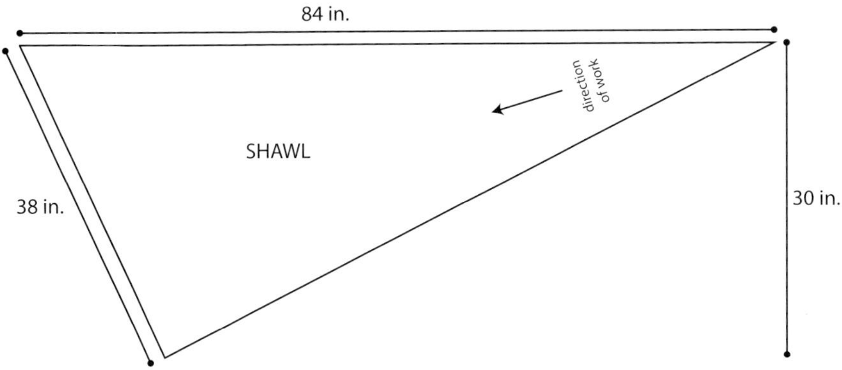

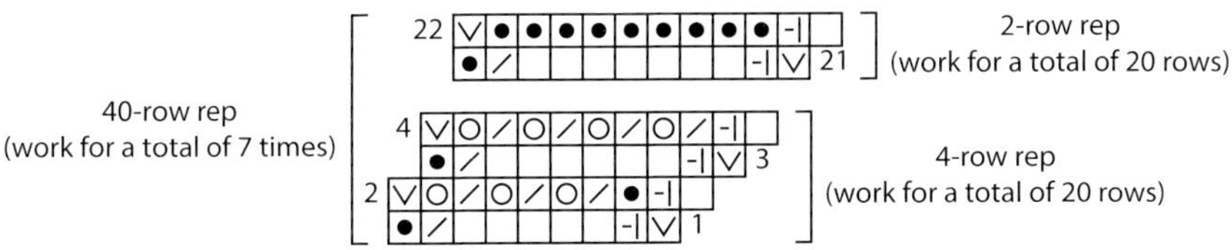

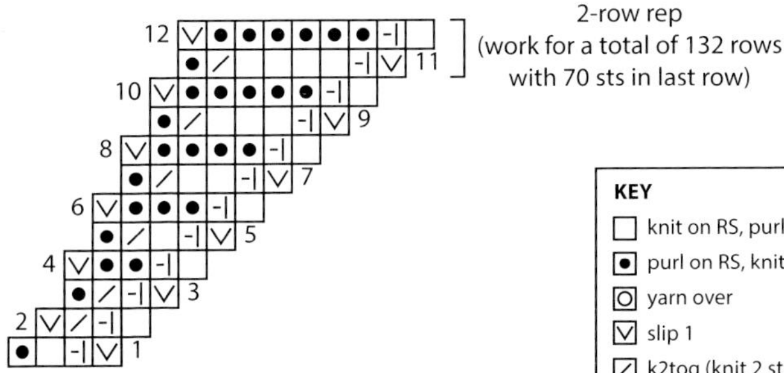

KEY

- ☐ knit on RS, purl on WS
- ● purl on RS, knit on WS
- ○ yarn over
- V slip 1
- / k2tog (knit 2 stitches together)
- -| kfb

LION BRAND® FERRIS WHEEL

North Oak Knit Scarf

●●○○ **EASY**

SIZE

About 8 x 78 in. (20.5 x 198 cm)

GAUGE

20 sts = about 4 in. (10 cm) over pattern Rows 1 and 2.

BE SURE TO CHECK YOUR GAUGE.

MATERIALS

Yarn (Medium) MEDIUM 4

Lion Brand® FERRIS WHEEL (Art. #217)

- ☐ #601 Summer Day 2 cakes
- ☐ LION BRAND® knitting needles size 7 (4.5 mm)
- ☐ LION BRAND® large-eyed blunt needle

NOTES

1. Scarf is worked in one piece.
2. Slip all slip sts as if to purl, wyif.
3. With yarn in front (wyif) refers to the side of the work facing you as you work the row. To move yarn from front to back or back to front, bring yarn between your needles, begin careful not to wrap yarn over the needle.

SCARF

Cast on 40 sts.

Row 1 (RS): Sl 1, k38, p1.

Row 2: *Wyif, sl 1 as if to purl, k2; repeat from * to last st, purl the last st.

Rep Rows 1 and 2 until piece measures about 78 in. (198 cm) from beginning, end with a Row 1 as the last row you work.

Bind off.

FINISHING

Weave in ends.

LION BRAND® FERRIS WHEEL

Pelham Hat

●●○○ **EASY**

SIZE

Finished Circumference:
About 19 in. (48.5 cm), will stretch to fit a range of sizes

GAUGE

20 sts = about 4 in. (10 cm) in St st worked in the rnd (k every rnd).

BE SURE TO CHECK YOUR GAUGE.

MATERIALS

Yarn (Medium) MEDIUM 4

Lion Brand® FERRIS WHEEL (Art. #217)

- ☐ #601 Summer Day 1 cake
- ☐ Lion Brand® double pointed needles size 6 (4 mm), set of 5
- ☐ Lion Brand® stitch markers
- ☐ Lion Brand® large-eyed blunt needle

Additional Materials

Circular knitting needle size 5 (3.75 mm), 16 in. (40.5 cm)

Circular knitting needle size 6 (4 mm), 16 in. (40.5 cm) long

NOTES

1. Hat is worked from lower edge up to crown (top of Hat).
2. Hat is worked in the round, beginning with a circular needle, then changing to double pointed needles (dpns) when sts have been sufficiently decreased.

PATTERN STITCH

K2, p2 Rib worked in the rnd (over a multiple of 4 sts)

Rnd 1: *K2, p2; rep from * around.

Rep Rnd 1 for K2, p2 Rib worked in the rnd.

HAT

With smaller circular needle, cast on 96 sts.

Place marker for beg of rnd. Join by working the first st on the left hand needle with the working yarn from the right hand needle and being careful not to twist sts.

Rnd 1: *K2, p2; rep from * around.

Rep Rnd 1 until piece measures about 3 in. (7.5 cm) from beg.

Change to larger circular needle and St st worked in the rnd (k every rnd) and work until piece measures about 8 in. (20.5 cm) from beg.

Shape Crown (top of Hat)

NOTE: When you place the markers on the next rnd, use different color markers than you used for the beg of the rnd marker.

Next (Decrease) Rnd: *K10, k2tog, place marker; rep from * 6 more times, k to last 2 sts before end of rnd marker, k2tog – 88 sts at the end of this rnd.

Next Rnd: Knit.

Next (Decrease) Rnd: *K to 2 sts before next marker, k2tog; rep from * around – 80 sts at the end of this rnd.

Next Rnd: Knit.

Rep last Decrease Rnd once more – you will have 72 sts (9 sts between each set of st markers).

Next Rnd: Knit, changing to double pointed needles (dpn) as follows: With first dpn, k18 sts from circular needle; with second, third and fourth dpn, k18 from circular needle. You will have 4 dpn with 18 sts on each.

Next (Decrease) Rnd: *K to 2 sts before next marker, k2tog; rep from * around – 64 sts at the end of this rnd.

Next Rnd: Knit.

Rep last 2 rnds until you have 16 sts remaining.

Next (Decrease) Rnd: *K2tog; rep from * to end of rnd – 8 sts.

Cut yarn, leaving a long yarn tail. Thread tail through remaining sts and pull to gather. Knot securely.

FINISHING

Weave in ends.

LION BRAND® MANDALA® THICK & QUICK®

Egg Harbor Afghan

●○○○ **BEGINNER**

SIZE

About 36 x 45½ in.
(91.5 x 115.5 cm)

GAUGE

8½ sts = about 4 in. (10 cm) over pattern Rows 1 and 2.

BE SURE TO CHECK YOUR GAUGE.

MATERIALS

Yarn (Super Bulky) SUPER BULKY 6

Lion Brand® MANDALA® THICK & QUICK® (Art. #528)

- ☐ #215 Garden Maze 2 cakes (A)
- ☐ #209 Thumbprint 2 cakes (B)
- ☐ #208 Turbine 1 cake (C)
- ☐ #214 Begonia 1 cake (D)
- ☐ #211 Pocket Watch 1 cake (E)
- ☐ Lion Brand® large-eyed blunt needle

Additional Materials

Circular knitting needle size 13 (9 mm), 36 in. (91.5 cm) long

NOTES

1. Afghan is worked in one piece with 5 colors of yarn.
2. A circular needle is used to accommodate the number of stitches. Work back and forth on the circular needle as if working on straight needles.

AFGHAN

With A, cast on 75 sts.

With A, knit 6 rows.

Row 1: With A, knit 4, purl to last 4 sts, knit 4.

Row 2: With A, knit.

With A, repeat Rows 1 and 2 until almost all of one ball of A has been used.

You will now be simply repeating Rows 1 and 2, changing yarn color each time you finish one ball of yarn.

Each color yarn will add about 6½ in. (16.5 cm) to the length of your Afghan.

TIP: To keep the edges of your Afghan neat, change the yarn color by working the first 4 sts with the old color yarn, then change to the new color. Leave 4-6 in. (10-15 cm) yarn tails on both the old and the new yarn colors.

The first and last 4 sts on the Afghan create side borders. After you've finished knitting the Afghan, weave in the yarn tails along the edge of the border.

Change yarn color as follows:

Use all of one ball of yarn color B.

Use all of each ball of C, D, and E.

Use all of the second ball of yarn color A.

Change to the second ball of B, and continue to repeat Rows 1 and 2 until this B section measures about 4½ in. (11.5 cm), end with a Row 2 as the last row you work.

With B, knit 6 rows.

Bind off loosely.

FINISHING

Weave in ends.

LION BRAND® SHAWL IN A CAKE

Light 'N Easy Cardigan

●●○○ **EASY**

SIZES

S (M/L, 1X-3X)

Finished Bust:
About 38 (46, 54) in.
(96.5 (117, 137) cm)

Finished Length:
About 18½ (20, 21) in.
[47 (51, 53.5) cm]

Note: Pattern is written for smallest size with changes for larger sizes in parentheses. When only one number is given, it applies to all sizes. To follow pattern more easily, circle all numbers pertaining to your size before beginning.

GAUGE

16 sts + 24 rows = about 4 in. (10 cm) in Rev St st (p on RS, k on WS).

BE SURE TO CHECK YOUR GAUGE.

MATERIALS

Yarn (Medium) MEDIUM 4

Lion Brand® SHAWL IN A CAKE (Art. #455)

- ☐ #300 Om Opal 2 (3, 4) cakes
- ☐ LION BRAND® stitch holders
- ☐ LION BRAND® large-eyed blunt needle

Additional Materials

Circular knitting needle size 7 (4.5 mm), 36 in. (91.5 cm) long

Circular knitting needle size 8 (5 mm), 36 in. (91.5 cm) long

NOTES

1. Cardigan is worked in 2 Halves. The Halves are sewn together at center back to make the Cardigan.
2. Each Half is worked side to side from sleeve to center back.
3. Halves are worked in Rev St st (p on RS, k on WS) with Garter st (k every row) borders.
4. Circular needles are used to accommodate the large number of sts. Work back and forth in rows on the circular needle as if working with straight needles.

STITCH EXPLANATIONS

M1P (make 1 st as if to purl)
An increase worked by lifting the horizontal strand lying between the needles and placing it onto the left needle. Purl this new stitch through the back loop – 1 st increased.

ssk (slip, slip, knit) Slip next 2 sts as if to knit, one at a time, to right needle; insert left needle into fronts of these 2 sts and knit them together – 1 st decreased.

LEFT HALF

Sleeve

With larger needle, cast on 42 (44, 46) sts.

Rows 1-10: Work in Garter st (k every row) for 10 rows.

Row 11 (Increase Row – RS): P1, M1P, p to last st, M1P, p1 – you will have 44 (46, 48) sts.

Rows 12-16: Beginning with a WS (knit) row, work in Rev St st (p on RS, k on WS) for 5 rows.

Rows 17-88 (100, 112): Rep Rows 11-16 for 12 (14, 16) more times – 68 (74, 80) sts.

Body

Row 1 (RS): Cast on 44 (46, 48) sts; beg over sts just cast on, k8, p to end of row – 112 (120, 128) sts.

Row 2: Cast on 44 (46, 48) sts; beg over sts just cast on, k to end of row – 156 (166, 176) sts.

Row 3: K8, p to last 8 sts, k8.

Row 4: Knit.

Rep Rows 3 and 4 until piece measures about 6 (7½, 9) in. **[**15 (19, 23) cm**]** from cast on sts of body, end with a RS row as the last row you work.

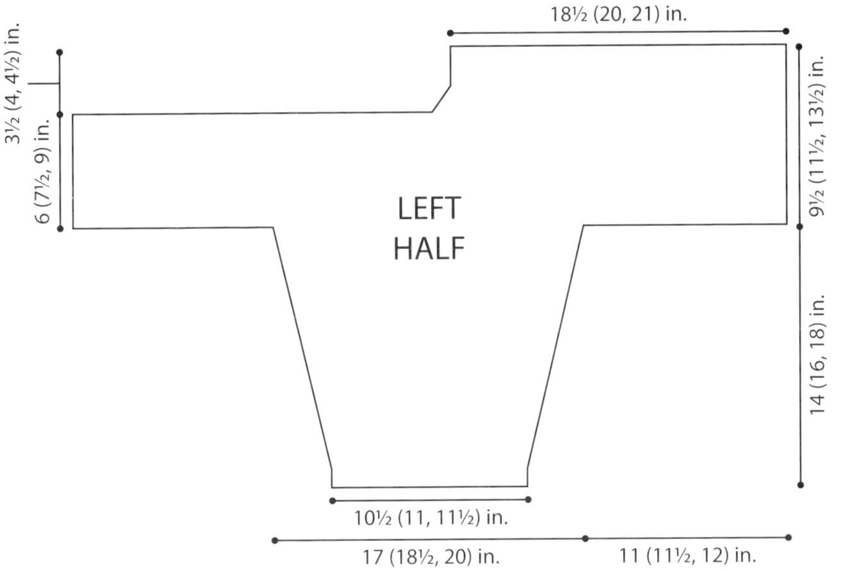
18½ (20, 21) in.
3½ (4, 4½) in.
6 (7½, 9) in.
LEFT HALF
9½ (11½, 13½) in.
14 (16, 18) in.
10½ (11, 11½) in.
17 (18½, 20) in.
11 (11½, 12) in.

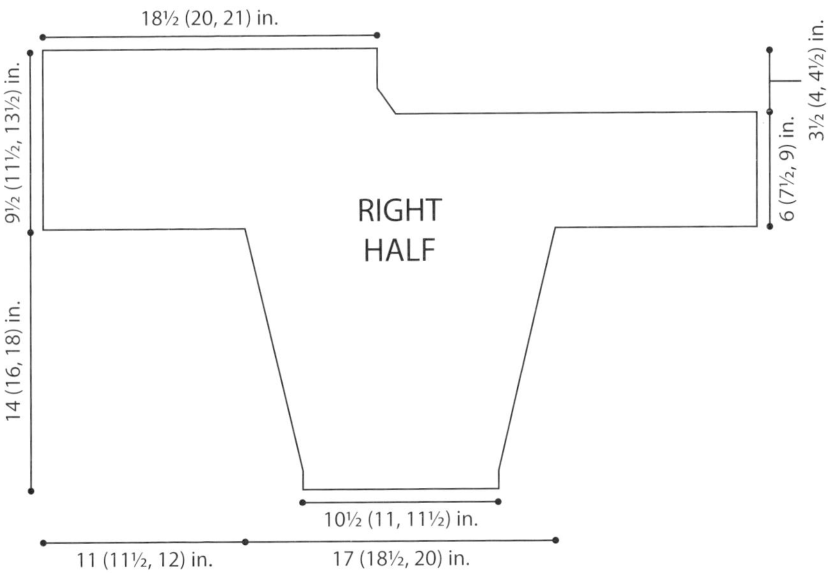
18½ (20, 21) in.
9½ (11½, 13½) in.
RIGHT HALF
3½ (4, 4½) in.
6 (7½, 9) in.
14 (16, 18) in.
10½ (11, 11½) in.
11 (11½, 12) in.
17 (18½, 20) in.

Shape Neck

Row 1 (WS): K78 (83, 88) sts and place these sts on a st holder for left front edge sts, k to end of row – 78 (83, 88) sts rem on needle.

Row 2: K8, p to end of row.

Row 3 (Decrease Row): K1, ssk, k to end of row – 77 (82, 87) sts.

Rows 4-9: Rep Rows 2 and 3 for 3 more times – 74 (79, 84) sts in Row 9.

Row 10: K8, p to end of row.

Row 11: Knit.

Rep Rows 10 and 11 until piece measures about 9½ (11½, 13½) in. **[**24 (29, 34.5) cm**]** from cast on sts of body.

Bind off.

RIGHT HALF

Work same as Left Half to Shape Neck, end with a WS row as the last row you work.

Shape Neck

Row 1 (RS): K8, p70 (75, 80) sts and place these last 78 (83, 88) sts on a st holder for front edge sts, p to last 8 sts, k8 – 78 (83, 88) sts rem on needle.

Row 2: Knit.

Row 3 (Decrease Row): P1, p2tog, p to last 8 sts, k8 – 77 (82, 87) sts.

Rows 4-9: Rep Rows 2 and 3 for 3 more times – 74 (79, 84) sts in Row 9.

Row 10: Knit.

Row 11: P to last 8 sts, k8.

Rep Rows 10 and 11 until piece measures same length as Left Half.

Bind off.

FINISHING

Sew Halves together at center back.

Front Band

From RS, with smaller needle, k78 (83, 88) right front edge sts from st holder, pick up and k25 (31, 37) sts evenly spaced along back neck edge, k78 (83, 88) left front edge sts from st holder – 181 (197, 213) sts.

Work in Garter st for about 3 in. (7.5 cm).

With larger needle, bind off loosely.

Sew side and sleeve seams.

Weave in ends.

LION BRAND® SHAWL IN A CAKE

Breath of Glitter Shawl

●●○○ **EASY**

SIZE

About 17 x 54 in. (43 x 137 cm)

GAUGE

15 sts = about 4 in. (10 cm) in pattern.

BE SURE TO CHECK YOUR GAUGE.

MATERIALS

Yarn (Medium) MEDIUM 4

Lion Brand® SHAWL IN A CAKE (Art. #455)

☐ #303 Namaste Neutrals 1 cake

☐ LION BRAND® knitting needles size 10.5 (6.5 mm)

☐ LION BRAND® large-eyed blunt needle

NOTE

1. Shawl is worked in one piece in a very easy lace pattern.

STITCH EXPLANATIONS

Yo (yarn over)

An increase that also creates a small decorative hole (eyelet) in the fabric, worked as follows:

1. Bring yarn to front, between the needles.

2. Take yarn to back, over the right hand needle. This creates the new st. You are now ready to proceed with the next st as instructed.

Sk2p (slip-k2tog-pass slipped st over)

A double decrease worked as follows:

1. Insert right needle as if to knit, and slip the next st from the left hand needle to the right hand needle.

2. Knit the next 2 sts together.

3. With tip of left hand needle, lift the slipped st (the 2nd st on right needle) up and over the k2tog (first st on right needle) and off the needle – you have decreased 2 sts.

SHAWL

Cast on 65 sts.

Row 1 (wrong side): K2, purl to last 2 sts, k2.

Row 2 (right side): K3, *yo, k1, sk2p, k1, yo, k1; rep from* to last 2 sts, k2.

Rep Rows 1 and 2 until about 2 yds. (2 m) of yarn remains.

Bind off.

FINISHING

Weave in ends.

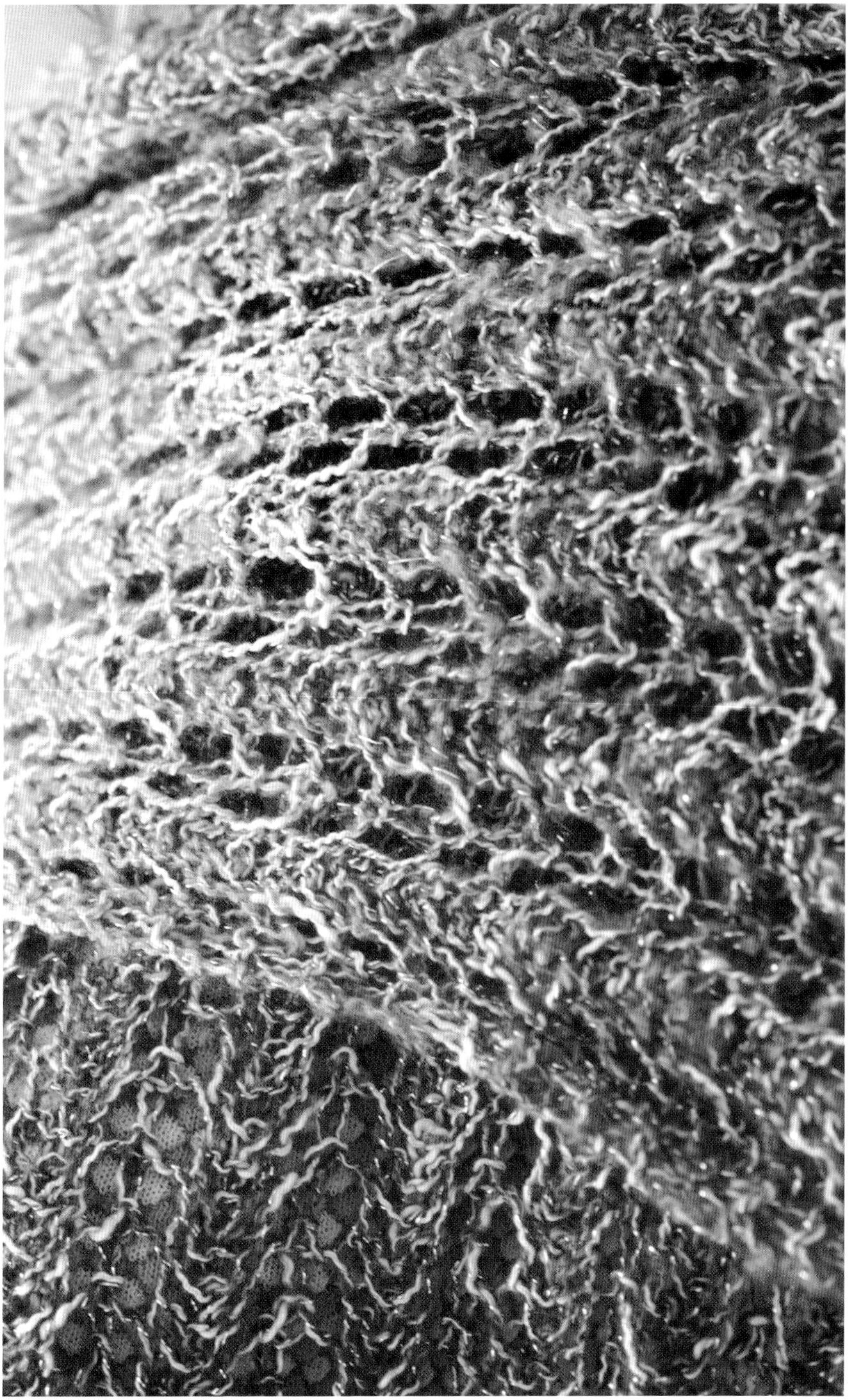

LION BRAND® COBOO

Beach Haven Shawl

●●○○ **EASY**

SIZE

Finished Curved Top Edge:
About 64 in. (162.5 cm)

Finished Length at Center Back:
About 21 in. (53.5 cm)

GAUGE

18 sts + 24 rows = about 4 in. (10 cm) in Stockinette st (k on RS, p on WS).

BE SURE TO CHECK YOUR GAUGE.

MATERIALS

LIGHT 3

Yarn (Light)

Lion Brand® COBOO (Art. #835)

- ☐ #107 Denim 1 cake (A)
- ☐ #109 Steel Blue 1 cake (B)
- ☐ #106 Ice Blue 1 cake (C)
- ☐ #149 Silver 1 cake (D)
- ☐ Lion Brand® stitch markers
- ☐ Lion Brand® large-eyed blunt needle

Additional Materials

Circular knitting needle size 7 (4.5 mm), 36 in. (91.5 cm) long

NOTES

1. Shawl is worked in one piece from back neck downwards.
2. After the first few rows, 4 rows of Stockinette st (k on RS, p on WS) alternate with 6 rows of Garter st (k every st of every row) and Eyelet Rows are worked every 10th then every 20th row.
3. Yarn over increases are worked to shape the Shawl.
4. The first st of every row is slipped and the last st is purled. This creates neat edges on the Shawl.
5. When the pattern tells you to slip a st, slip as if to knit or as if to purl, whichever look you prefer.
6. A circular needle is used to accommodate the number of sts. Work back and forth in rows on the circular needle as if working on straight needles.

STITCH EXPLANATION

yo (yarn over)

An increase that also creates a small decorative hole (eyelet) in the fabric, worked as follows:

1. Bring yarn to front, between the needles.

2. Take yarn to back, over the right needle. This creates the new st. You are now ready to proceed with the next st as instructed.

SHAWL

With A, cast on 3 sts.

Row 1 (RS): Sl 1, yo, k1, yo, p1 – you will have 5 sts in this row.

Row 2: Sl 1, k3, p1.

Row 3: Sl 1, yo, k3, yo, p1 – 7 sts.

Row 4: Sl 1, k5, p1.

Row 5 (Eyelet Row): Sl 1, *yo, k1; rep from * to last st, yo, p1 – 13 sts.

Row 6: Sl 1, p to end of row.

Row 7: Sl 1, yo, k to last st, yo, p1 – 15 sts.

Row 8: Sl 1, p to end of row.

Row 9: Sl 1, yo, k to last st, yo, p1 – 17 sts.

Row 10: Sl 1, k to last st, p1.

Rows 11-14: Rep Rows 9 and 10 twice – 21 sts in Row 13.

Rows 15-24: Rep Rows 5-14 – 49 sts in Row 23.

Row 25 (Eyelet Row): Sl 1, *yo, k2; rep from * to last 4 sts, yo, k3, yo, p1 – 73 sts.

Rows 26-34: Rep Rows 6-14 – 81 sts in Row 33.

Row 35: Sl 1, yo, k to last st, yo, p1 – 83 sts.

Rows 36-44: Rep Rows 6-14 – 91 sts in Row 43.

Row 45 (Eyelet Row): Sl 1, *yo, k3; rep from * to last 3 sts, k2, yo, p1 – 121 sts.

Rows 46-54: Rep Rows 6-14 – 129 sts in Row 53.

Rows 55-74: Rep Rows 35-54 – 193 sts in Row 73.

Row 75: Sl 1, yo, k to last st, yo, p1 – 195 sts.

Rows 76-78: Rep Rows 6-8 – 197 sts in Row 77.

Change to B.

Rows 79-84: Rep Rows 9-14 – 203 sts in Row 83.

Row 85 (Eyelet Row): Sl 1, *yo, k4; rep from * to last 2 sts, k1, yo, p1 – 254 sts.

Rows 86-94: Rep Rows 6-14 – 262 sts in Row 93.

Rows 95-104: Rep Rows 35-44 – 272 sts in Row 103.

Row 105 (Eyelet Row): Sl 1, *yo, k4; rep from * to last 3 sts, k2, yo, p1 – 340 sts.

Rows 106-108: Rep Rows 6-8 – 342 sts in Row 107.

Change to C.

Rows 109-114: Rep Rows 9-14 – 348 sts in Row 113.

Row 115-124: Rep Rows 35-44 – 358 sts in Row 123.

Row 125 (Eyelet Row): Sl 1, *yo, k6; rep from * to last 3 sts, k2, yo, p1 – 418 sts.

Rows 126-134: Rep Rows 6-14 – 426 sts in Row 133.

Change to D.

Rows 135-144: Rep Rows 35-44 – 436 sts in Row 143.

Row 145 (Eyelet Row): Sl 1, *yo, k6; rep from * to last 3 sts, k2, yo, p1 – 509 sts.

Rows 146-154: Rep Rows 6-14 – 517 sts in Row 153.

Bind off.

FINISHING

Weave in ends.

LION BRAND® CUPCAKE®

Striped Triangle Shawl

●●○○ **EASY+**

SIZE

Finished Wingspan:
About 69 in. (175.5 cm)

Finished Length:
About 34 in. (86.5 cm), measured from top edge to lower point

GAUGE

18½ sts + 36 rows = about 4 in. (10 cm) in Garter st (k every st on every row)

BE SURE TO CHECK YOUR GAUGE.

MATERIALS

Yarn (Light) LIGHT 3

Lion Brand® CUPCAKE® (Art. #935)

- ☐ #210 Clown Car 2 cakes (A)
- ☐ #218 Tutu Much 1 cake (B)
- ☐ LION BRAND® stitch markers
- ☐ LION BRAND® large-eyed blunt needle

Additional Materials

Circular knitting needle size 5 (3.75 mm), 36 in. (91.5 cm) long

NOTES

1. Shawl is made in one piece, beginning with a triangle.
2. After the first Triangle is made, sts are picked up along edge(s) of previous Triangles to begin the next Triangle.
3. All Triangles are worked back and forth in rows and shaped with decreases.
4. Refer to our diagram to clarify the construction of the Shawl.
5. A circular needle is used to accommodate the sts. Work back and forth in rows on the circular needle as if working on straight needles.
6. After the first few rows, the yarn color is changed every 4 rows to make stripes.
7. To create neat edges, the first st of every row is slipped and the last st is purled. Slip sts as if to purl or as if to knit, whichever you prefer.

STITCH EXPLANATION

ssk (slip, slip, knit)

Slip next 2 sts as if to knit, one at a time, to right needle; insert left needle into fronts of these 2 sts and knit them together – 1 st decreased.

TECHNIQUE EXPLANATION

Cable Cast On

*Insert right needle between first 2 sts on left needle, wrap yarn and pull through (as if knitting a st), transfer new st to left needle; rep from * for desired number of sts.

SHAWL

Triangle I

With A, cast on 232 sts.

Row 1 (WS): With A, sl 1 (edge st), k115, place marker (pm) for center, k115, p1 (edge st).

Row 2 (Decrease Row – RS): With A, sl 1, k2tog, k to 3 sts before marker, ssk, k1, slip marker (sm), k1, k2tog, k to last 3 sts, ssk, p1 – you will have 228 sts in this row.

Row 3: With A, sl 1, k to last st slipping marker as you come to it, p1.

Rows 4-7: With B, rep Rows 2 and 3 twice – 220 sts in Row 6.

Rows 8-11: With A, rep Rows 2 and 3 twice – 212 sts in Row 10.

Rows 12-107: Rep Rows 4-11 for 12 times – 20 sts in Row 106.

Rows 108-111: Rep Rows 4-7 – 12 sts in Row 110.

Row 112: With A, rep Row 2 – 8 sts.

Row 113: With A, sl 1, k1, k2tog, pass knit st over k2tog and off needle, sm, k1, k2tog, pass knit st over k2tog and off needle, p1 – 4 sts.

Row 114: With A, k2tog, sm, k2tog – 2 sts.

Row 115: With A, k2tog, removing center marker.

Fasten off last st.

Place marker on last st.

Triangle II

With A, cast on 80 sts.

From RS and working across first half of top edge of Triangle I, pick up and k80 sts evenly spaced between right corner and center marker – 160 sts.

TIPS:

Refer to the diagram for which edge of the triangle to pick up along.

To pick up 80 sts evenly spaced along an edge, use stitch markers to divide the edge into 4 equal sections then pick up and knit 20 sts in each section.

Row 1 (WS): With A, sl 1, k79, pm for center, k to last st, p1.

Row 2 (Decrease Row – RS): With A, sl 1, k2tog, k to 3 sts before marker, ssk, k1, sm, k1, k2tog, k to last 3 sts, ssk, p1 – 156 sts.

Row 3: With A, sl 1, k to last st slipping marker as you come to it, p1.

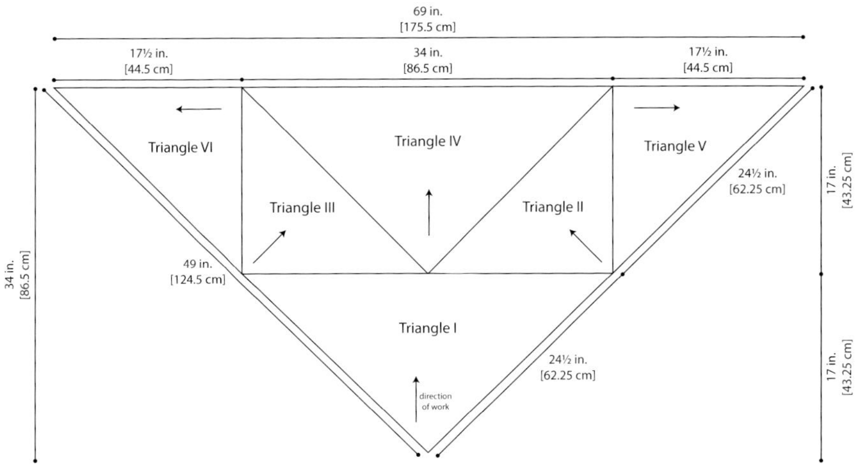
69 in.
[175.5 cm]
17½ in.
[44.5 cm]
34 in.
[86.5 cm]
17½ in.
[44.5 cm]
Triangle VI
Triangle IV
Triangle V
Triangle III
Triangle II
24½ in.
[62.25 cm]
17 in.
[43.25 cm]
34 in.
[86.5 cm]
49 in.
[124.5 cm]
Triangle I
24½ in.
[62.25 cm]
17 in.
[43.25 cm]
direction
of work

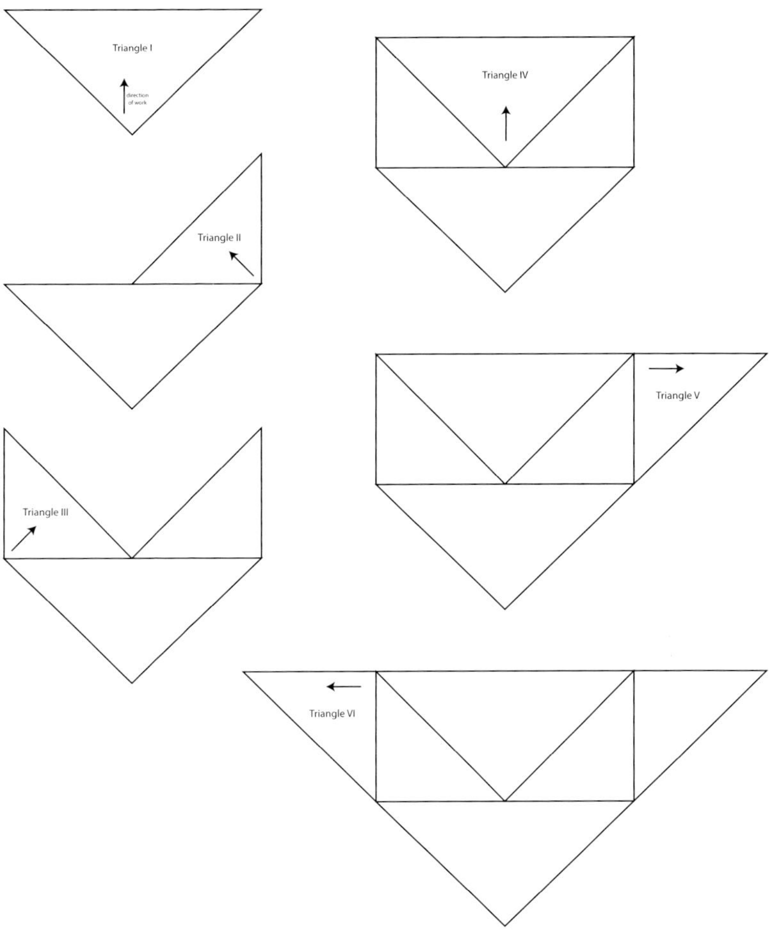
Triangle I
direction
of work
Triangle IV
Triangle II
Triangle V
Triangle III
Triangle VI

Rows 4-7: With B, rep Rows 2 and 3 twice – 148 sts in Row 6.

Rows 8-11: With A, rep Rows 2 and 3 twice – 140 sts in Row 10.

Rows 12-75: Rep Rows 4-11 for 8 times – 12 sts in Row 74.

Row 76: With B, rep Row 2 – 8 sts.

Row 77: With B, sl 1, k1, k2tog, pass knit st over k2tog and off needle, sm, k1, k2tog, pass knit st over k2tog and off needle, p1 – 4 sts.

Row 78: With B, k2tog, sm, k2tog – 2 sts.

Row 79: With B, k2tog, removing center marker.

Fasten off last st.

Triangle III

From RS with A, and working across rem top edge of Triangle I, pick up and k80 sts evenly spaced between center marker and left corner, using Cable Cast-On, cast on 80 sts – 160 sts.

Rows 1-79: Work same as Rows 1-79 of Triangle II.

Fasten off last st.

Triangle IV

From RS with A, pick up and k116 sts evenly spaced along top edge of Triangle II then pick up and k116 sts evenly spaced along top edge of Triangle III – 232 sts.

Rows 1-115: Work same as Rows 1-115 of Triangle I.

Fasten off last st.

Triangle V

NOTE: Wind remaining yarn A into 2 separate balls so that each ball begins with a different color. For Triangles V and VI use the 2nd ball of A for yarn color C.

From RS with A, pick up and k80 sts evenly spaced along side edge of Triangle II – 80 sts.

Row 1 (WS): With A, sl 1, k to last st, p1.

Row 2: With A, sl 1, k2tog, k to last st, p1 – 79 sts.

Row 3: With A, sl 1, k to last st, p1.

Rows 4-7: With C, rep Rows 2 and 3 twice – 77 sts in Row 6.

Rows 8-11: With A, rep Rows 2 and 3 twice – 75 sts in Row 10.

Rows 12-155: Rep Rows 4-11 for 18 times – 3 sts in Row 154.

Row 156: With C, sl 1, k2tog – 2 sts.

Row 157: With C, k2tog.

Fasten off last st.

Triangle VI

From RS with A, pick up and k80 sts evenly spaced along side edge of Triangle III – 80 sts.

Row 1 (WS): With A, sl 1, k to last st, p1.

Row 2: With A, sl 1, k to last 3 sts, ssk, p1 – 79 sts.

Row 3: With A, sl 1, k to last st, p1.

Rows 4-7: With C, rep Rows 2 and 3 twice – 77 sts in Row 6.

Rows 8-11: With A, rep Rows 2 and 3 twice – 75 sts in Row 10.

Rows 12-155: Rep Rows 4-11 for 18 times – 3 sts in Row 154.

Row 156: With C, sl 1, k2tog – 2 sts.

Row 157: With C, k2tog.

Fasten off last st.

FINISHING

Weave in ends.

LION BRAND® MANDALA® SPARKLE

Urbana Cowl

●○○○ **BEGINNER**

SIZE

Finished Circumference:
About 60 in. (152.5 cm)

Finished Height:
About 7½ in. (19 cm)

GAUGE

18 sts = about 4 in. (10 cm) over Rows 1 and 2.

BE SURE TO CHECK YOUR GAUGE.

MATERIALS

Yarn (Light) LIGHT 3

Lion Brand® MANDALA® SPARKLE (Art. #527)

- ☐ #312 Crux 1 cake
- ☐ Lion Brand® knitting needles size 6 (4 mm)
- ☐ Lion Brand® large-eyed blunt needle

NOTE

Cowl is worked in one piece and then seamed to make a ring.

COWL

Cast on 33 sts.

Row 1: Knit.

Row 2: Knit 3, *purl 3, knit 3; repeat from * to end of row.

Repeat Rows 1 and 2 until only about 2 yd. (2 m) of yarn remains.

Bind off, but do not cut yarn.

FINISHING

Thread yarn tail into blunt needle.

Sew cast-on and bound-off ends of piece together to make a ring.

Weave in ends.

LION BRAND® CUPCAKE®

Easy Triangle Shawl

●●○○ **EASY**

SIZE

About 17 x 73 in. (43 x 185.5 cm), at widest and longest

GAUGE

18 sts = about 4 in. (10 cm) in Garter st (knit every st on every row).

BE SURE TO CHECK YOUR GAUGE.

MATERIALS

Yarn (Light) LIGHT 3

Lion Brand® CUPCAKE® (Art. #935)

- ☐ #214 Moody Blue 1 cake
- ☐ Lion Brand® large-eyed blunt needle

Additional Materials

Circular knitting needle size 5 (3.75 mm), 36 in. (91.5 cm) long

NOTES

1. Shawl is worked in one piece in Garter st (knit every st on every row) and shaped to make an asymmetric triangle.
2. The first st of every row is slipped for a neat edge. Slip the st as if to knit or as if to purl, whichever you prefer.
3. Increases are worked at the beginning of RS rows and end of WS rows and decreases are worked at the end of RS rows to shape the Shawl.
4. A circular needle is used to accommodate the large number of sts. Work back and forth on the circular needle as if you were working on straight needles.
5. For those who find a visual helpful, we have included a chart.

STITCH EXPLANATIONS

kfb (knit in front and back)

Knit next st without removing it from left hand needle, then k through back of same st – 1 st increased.

yo (yarn over)

An increase that also creates a small decorative hole (eyelet) in the fabric, worked as follows:

1. Bring yarn to front, between the needles.

2.. Take yarn to back, over the right hand needle. This creates the new st. You are now ready to proceed with the next st as instructed.

SHAWL

Cast on 4 sts.

Row 1 (RS): Sl 1, kfb, k1, p1 – you will have 5 sts in this row.

Row 2: Sl 1, k2tog, kfb, p1 – 5 sts.

Row 3: Sl 1, kfb, k2tog, p1.

Row 4: Sl 1, k to last 2 sts, kfb, p1 – 6 sts.

Row 5: Sl 1, kfb, k to last 3 sts, k2tog, p1.

Row 6: Sl 1, k to last 2 sts, kfb, p1 – 7 sts.

Rows 7-132: Rep Rows 5 and 6 until you have a total of 70 sts.

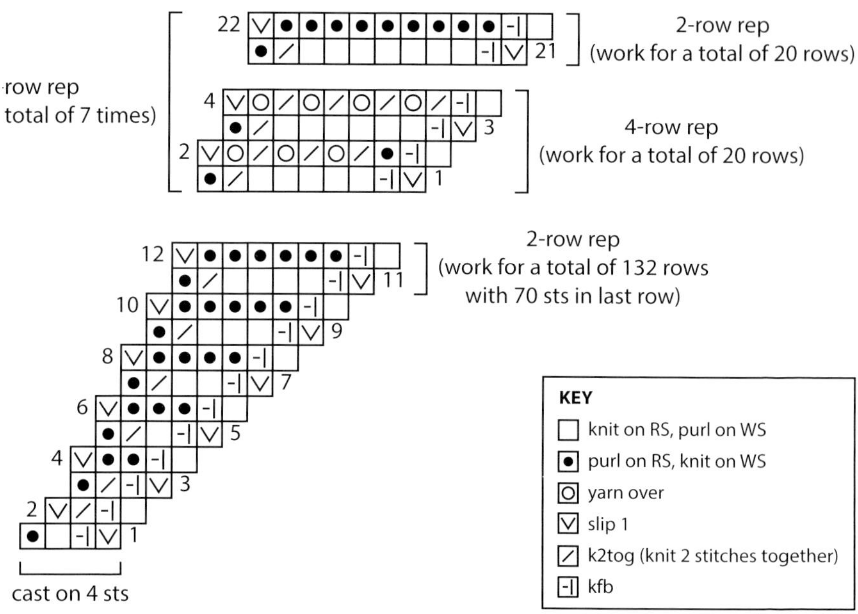

Begin Lace Section

Row 1 (RS): Sl 1, kfb, k to last 3 sts, k2tog, p1.

Row 2: Sl 1, *yo, k2tog; rep from * to last 3 sts, k1, kfb, p1 – 71 sts.

Row 3: Sl 1, kfb, k to last 3 sts, k2tog, p1.

Row 4: Sl 1, *yo, k2tog; rep from * to last 2 sts, kfb, p1 – 72 sts.

Rows 5-20: Rep Rows 1-4 for 4 more times – 80 sts at the end of Row 20.

Row 21: Sl 1, kfb, k to last 3 sts, k2tog, p1.

Row 22: Sl 1, k to last 2 sts, kfb, p1 – 81 sts.

Rows 23-40: Rep Rows 21 and 22 for 9 times – 90 sts at the end of Row 40.

Rows 41-160: Rep Rows 1-40 for 3 times more – 150 sts.

Rows 161-190: Rep Rows 1-30 – 165 sts.

Bind off.

FINISHING

Weave in ends.

General Instructions

ABBREVIATIONS

beg	begin(s)(ning)
cm	centimeters
dpn	double pointed needles
K	knit
kfb	knit in front and back
M1P	make one purl
m	meter(s)
mm	millimeters
P	purl
pm	place marker
rep	repeat(s)(ing)
Rev St st	Reverse Stockinette stitch
Rnd(s)	Round(s)
RS	right side
sl	slip
Sk2p	Slip-k2tog-pass slipped st over
sm	slip marker
SSK	slip, slip, knit
st(s)	stitch(es)
St st	Stockinette stitch
tbl	through back loop(s)
tog	together
WS	wrong side
wyif	with yarn in front
yd	yard(s)
YO	yarn over

KNIT TERMINOLOGY		
UNITED STATES		INTERNATIONAL
gauge	=	tension
bind off	=	cast off
yarn over (YO)	=	yarn forward (yfwd) **or** yarn around needle (yrn)

KNITTING NEEDLES		
UNITED STATES	ENGLISH U.K.	METRIC (mm)
0	13	2
1	12	2.25
2	11	2.75
3	10	3.25
4	9	3.5
5	8	3.75
6	7	4
7	6	4.5
8	5	5
9	4	5.5
10	3	6
10 1/2	2	6.5
11	1	8
13	00	9
15	000	10
17	---	12.75
19	---	15
35	---	19
50	---	25

●○○○ **BEGINNER**	Projects for first-time knitters using basic knit and purl stitches. Minimal shaping.
●●○○ **EASY**	Projects using basic stitches, repetitive stitch patterns, simple color changes, and simple shaping and finishing.
●●●○ **INTERMEDIATE**	Projects with a variety of stitches, such as basic cables and lace, simple intarsia, double-pointed needles and knitting in the round needle techniques, mid-level shaping and finishing.
●●●● **EXPERIENCED**	Projects using advanced techniques and stitches, such as short rows, fair isle, more intricate intarsia, cables, lace patterns, and numerous color changes.

Yarn Weight Symbol & Names	LACE 0	SUPER FINE 1	FINE 2	LIGHT 3	MEDIUM 4	BULKY 5	SUPER BULKY 6	JUMBO 7
Type of Yarns in Category	Fingering, size 10 crochet thread	Sock, Fingering, Baby	Sport, Baby	DK, Light Worsted	Worsted, Afghan, Aran	Chunky, Craft, Rug	Super Bulky, Roving	Jumbo, Roving
Knit Gauge Ranges in Stockinette St to 4" (10 cm)	33-40 sts**	27-32 sts	23-26 sts	21-24 sts	16-20 sts	12-15 sts	7-11 sts	6 sts and fewer
Advised Needle Size Range	000 to 1	1 to 3	3 to 5	5 to 7	7 to 9	9 to11	11 to 17	17 and larger

* GUIDELINES ONLY: The chart above reflects the most commonly used gauges and needle sizes for specific yarn categories.

** Lace weight yarns are usually knitted on larger needles to create lacy openwork patterns. Accordingly, a gauge range is difficult to determine. Always follow the gauge stated in your pattern.

SYMBOLS & TERMS

* — work instructions following ★ as many **more** times as indicated in addition to the first time.

( ) or **[ ]** — contains explanatory remarks.

GAUGE

Exact gauge is **essential** for proper size. Before beginning your project, make a sample swatch in the yarn and needle specified in the individual instructions. After completing the swatch, measure it, counting your stitches and rows or rounds carefully. If your swatch is larger or smaller than specified, **make another, changing needle size to get the correct gauge**. Keep trying until you find the size needle(s) that will give you the specified gauge.

MARKERS

As a convenience to you, we have used markers to help distinguish the beginning of a round. Place markers as instructed. You may use a purchased marker or tie a length of contrasting color yarn around the needle. When you reach a marker on each round, slip it from the left needle to the right needle; remove it when no longer needed.

When using double pointed needles, a split-ring marker can be placed around the first stitch in the round to indicate the beginning of the round. Move it up as the first stitch of each round is worked.

KNITTING IN THE ROUND

Circular Needle

Using a circular needle, cast on all stitches as instructed. Untwist and straighten the stitches on the needle to be sure that the cast on ridge lays on the inside of the needle and never rolls around the needle.

Hold the needle so that the ball of yarn is attached to the stitch closest to the **right** hand point. Place a marker on the right hand point to mark the beginning of the round.

To begin working in the round, knit the stitches on the left hand point ***(Fig. 1)***.

Continue working each round as instructed **without turning the work**; but for the first three rounds or so, check to be sure that the cast on edge has not twisted around the needle. If it has, it is impossible to untwist it. The only way to fix this is to rip it out and return to the cast on row.

Fig. 1

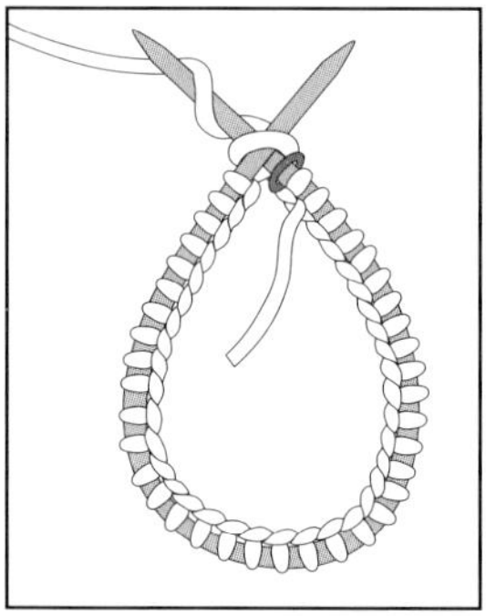

Double Pointed Needles

When working too few stitches to use a circular needle, double pointed needles are required. Divide the stitches into fourths and slip one-fourth of the stitches onto each of 4 double pointed needles ***(Fig. 2a)***. Being careful not to twist the cast on ridge, form a square with the needles ***(Fig. 2b)***. With the remaining needle, knit across the stitches on the first needle. You will now have an empty needle with which to knit the stitches from the next needle. Work the first stitch of each needle firmly to prevent gaps.

Fig. 2a

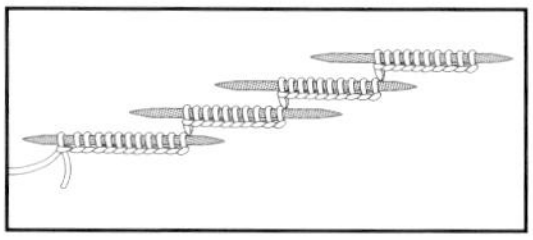

Fig. 2b

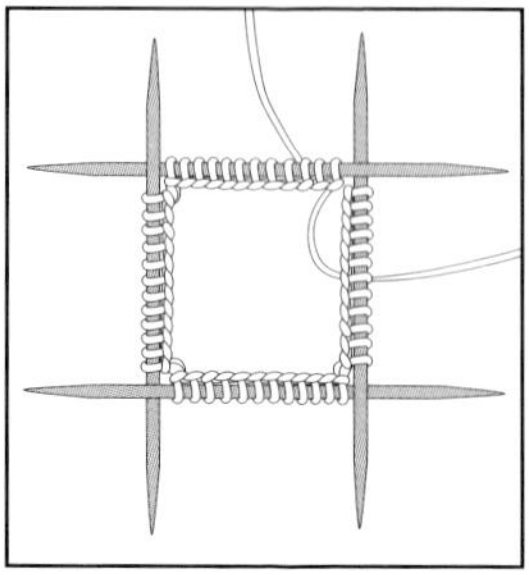

INCREASES

Cable Cast On

Insert the right needle from **front** to **back** between the first two stitches on the left needle, yarn over and pull up a loop ***(Fig. 3a)***, insert the left needle into the loop just worked from **front** to **back** and slip the loop onto the left needle ***(Fig. 3b)***. Repeat for the required number of stitches.

Fig. 3a

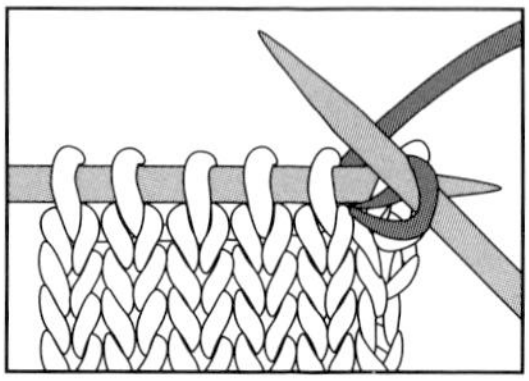

Fig. 3b

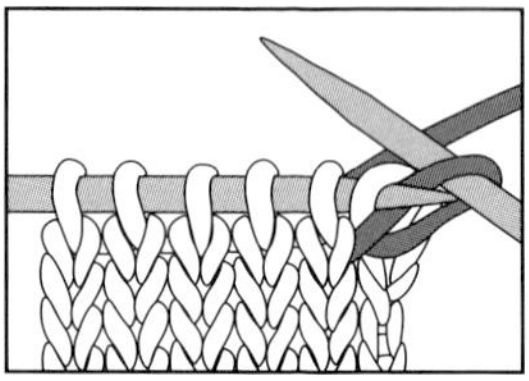

Knit in Front and Back

(abbreviated kfb)

Knit the next stitch but do **not** slip the old stitch off the left needle ***(Fig. 4a)***. Insert the right needle into the **back** loop of the **same** stitch and knit it ***(Fig. 4b)***, then slip the old stitch off the left needle.

Fig. 4a

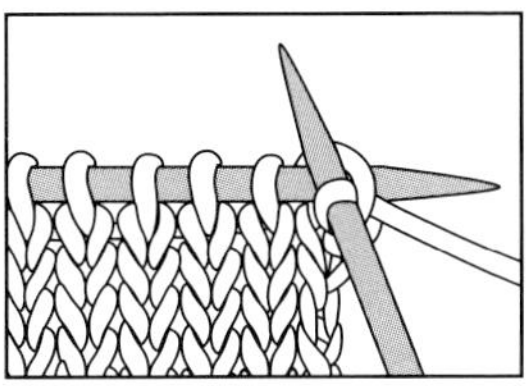

Fig. 4b

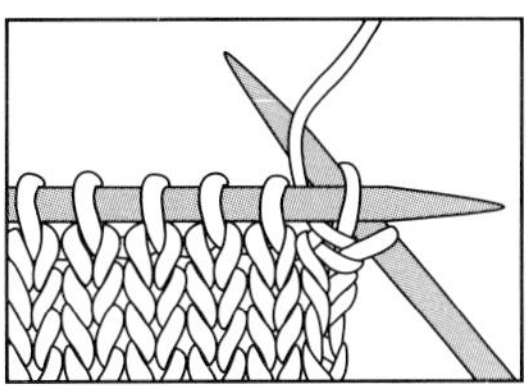

Yarn Over

(abbreviated YO)

After a knit stitch, before a knit stitch

Bring the yarn forward **between** the needles, then back **over** the top of the right hand needle, so that it is now in position to knit the next stitch ***(Fig. 5a)***.

Fig. 5a

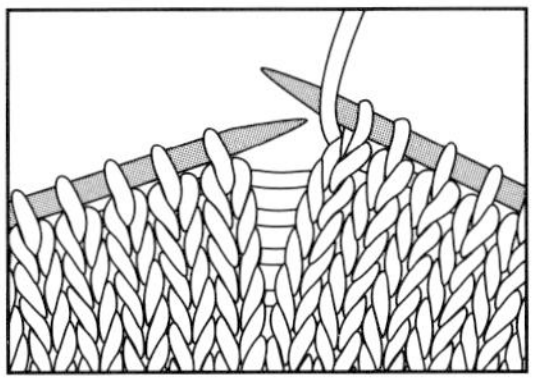

After a knit stitch, before a purl stitch

Bring the yarn forward **between** the needles, then back **over** the top of the right hand needle and forward **between** the needles again, so that it is now in position to purl the next stitch ***(Fig. 5b)***.

Fig. 5b

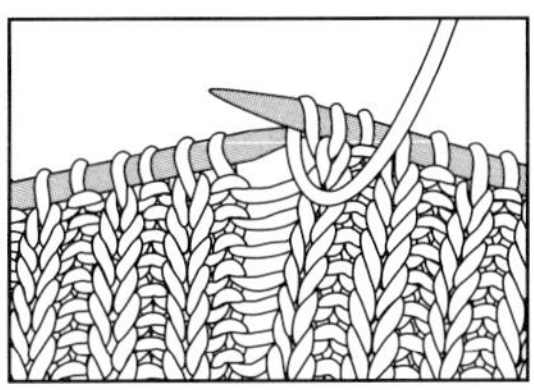

Make One Purl

(abbreviated M1P)

Insert the **left** needle under the horizontal strand between the stitches from the **front** ***(Fig. 6a)***. Then purl into the **back** of the strand ***(Fig. 6b)***.

Fig. 6a

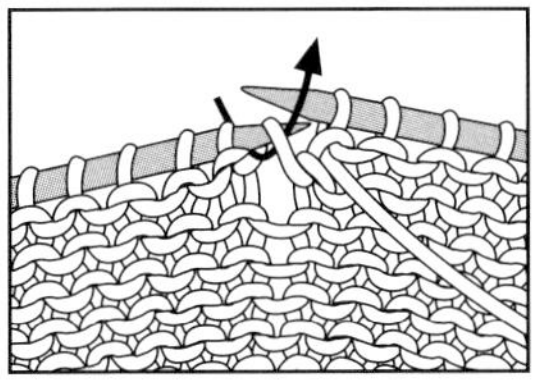

Fig. 6b

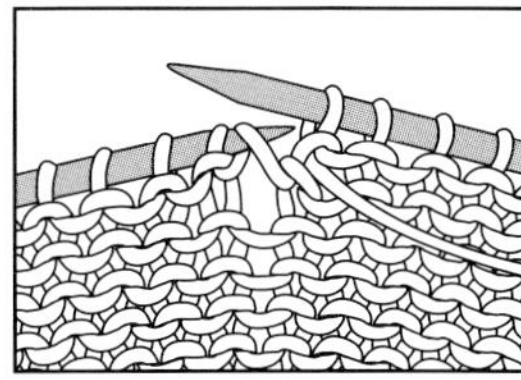

DECREASES

Knit 2 Together

(abbreviated K2tog)

Insert the right needle into the **front** of the first two stitches on the left needle as if to **knit** ***(Fig. 7)***, then **knit** them together as if they were one stitch.

Fig. 7

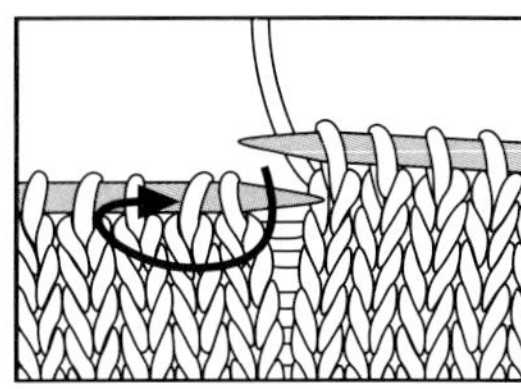

Purl 2 Together

(abbreviated P2tog)

Insert the right needle into the **front** of the first two stitches on the left needle as if to **purl** ***(Fig. 8)***, then **purl** them together as if they were one stitch.

Fig. 8

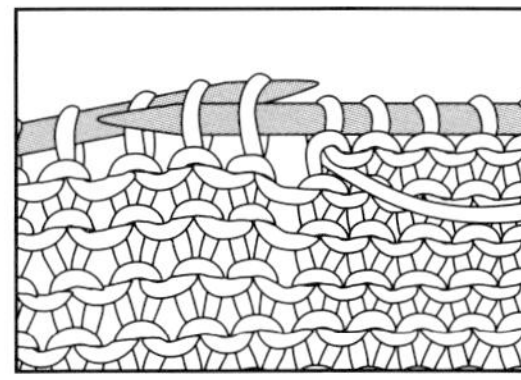

Slip 1, Knit 2 Together, Pass Slipped Stitch Over
(abbreviated Sk2p)

Slip one stitch as if to **knit** ***(Fig. 9a)***, then knit the next two stitches together ***(Fig.9)***. With the left needle, bring the slipped stitch over the stitch just made ***(Fig. 9b)*** and off the needle.

Fig. 9a

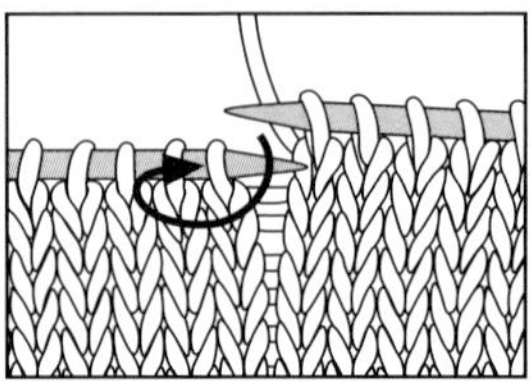

Fig. 9b

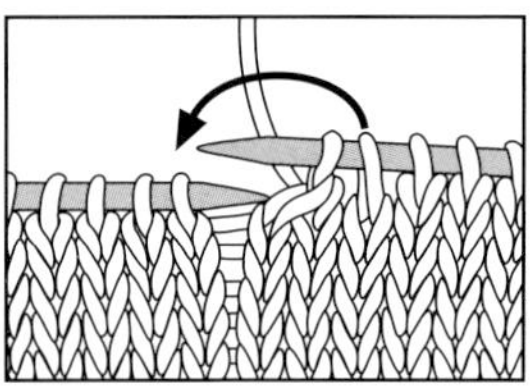

Slip, Slip, Knit
(abbreviated SSK)

Separately slip two stitches as if to knit ***(Fig. 10a)***. Insert the **left** needle into the **front** of both slipped stitches ***(Fig. 10b)*** and then **knit** them together as if they were one stitch ***(Fig. 10c)***.

Fig. 10a

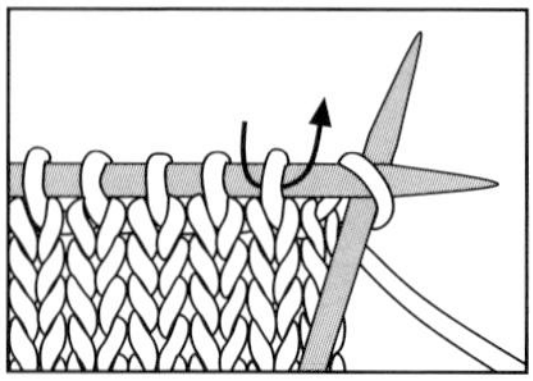

Fig. 10b

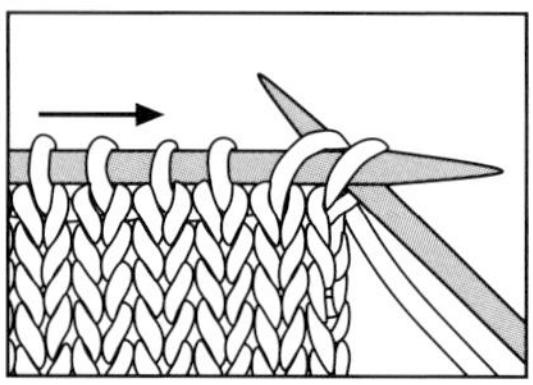

Fig. 10c

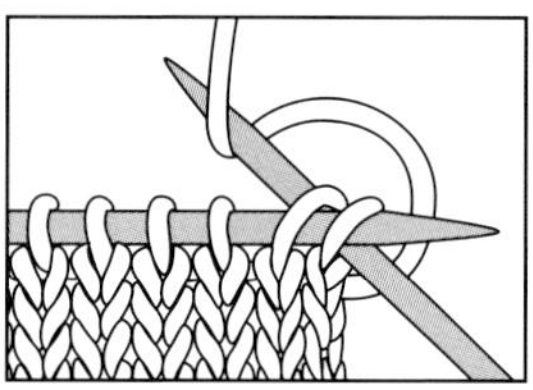

PICKING UP STITCHES

When instructed to pick up stitches, insert the needle from the **front** to the **back** under two strands at the edge of the worked piece ***(Figs. 11a & b)***. Put the yarn around the needle as if to **knit**, then bring the needle with the yarn back through the stitch to the right side, resulting in a stitch on the needle.

Repeat this along the edge, picking up the required number of stitches.

A crochet hook may be helpful to pull yarn through.

Fig. 11a

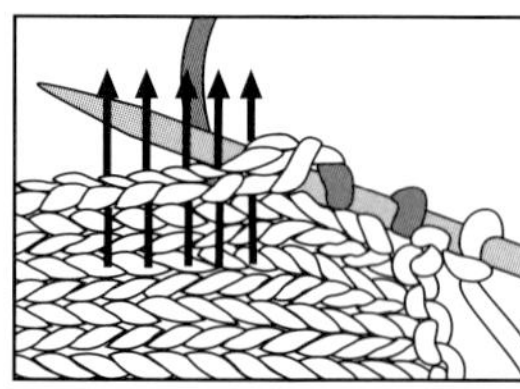

Fig. 11b

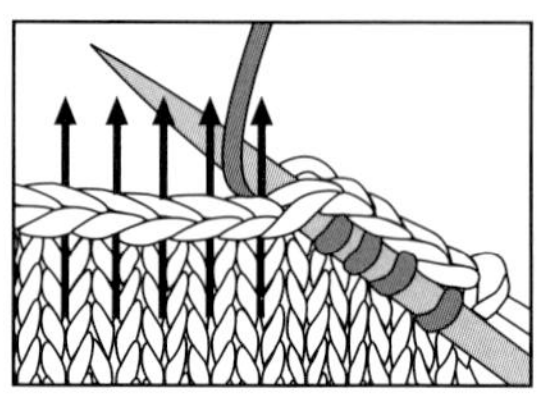

We have made every effort to ensure that these instructions are accurate and complete. We cannot, however, be responsible for human error, typographical mistakes, or variations in individual work.

Made in U.S.A.